This Book Belongs To

_____

_____

_____

Visit Us at
ChooseJoyPress.com
Sign up for our newsletter
& grab a free gift

He spoke about the kingdom of God, and taught the things about our Lord Jesus Christ with boldness, and he would not be stopped.

Acts 28:31

I am not afraid because I know God
is always with me.

-Isaiah 41:10

I believe God hears the cries of my heart
and answers them with love.

-2 Corinthians 6:2

I know God watches over me and keeps me safe from harm.

-Psalm 18:2

_____
_____
_____
_____
_____
_____
_____
_____
_____
_____
_____
_____
_____
_____
_____
_____

I am committed to God and trust that he will take care of all my needs.

-Psalm 31:14-15

_____
_____
_____
_____
_____
_____
_____
_____
_____
_____
_____

I pray daily for God's guidance.

-Colossians 2:7

_____
_____
_____
_____
_____
_____
_____
_____
_____
_____
_____
_____
_____
_____

I believe all things are possible with God
and that he guides my way.

-Jeremiah 32:17

I know that no matter what happens God gives me hope.

-Job 11:18

_____
_____
_____
_____
_____
_____
_____
_____
_____
_____
_____
_____

I know that some day I will face God as he
as promised.

-Acts 3:21

I am blessed by God in so many ways and some I may not even be aware of.

-Philemon 1:6

_____

_____

_____

_____

_____

_____

_____

_____

_____

_____

_____

_____

I am certain the Lord has shown me compassion and mercy.

-Psalm 103:8

I will always put my faith and trust in God and love him with all my heart.

-Proverbs 3:5-6

_____
_____
_____
_____
_____
_____
_____
_____
_____
_____
_____
_____
_____
_____

I lean on God when I'm afraid because I trust in his strength.

-Psalm 31:14-15

I am happy knowing Good is near and has
a hand upon my life even life is not easy.

-Psalm 145:3

_____
_____
_____
_____
_____
_____
_____
_____
_____
_____
_____
_____
_____

I give God my mind heart and soul every day, as he requests.

-Proverbs 4:23

_____
_____
_____
_____
_____
_____
_____
_____
_____
_____
_____
_____
_____

I thank God for this day and his grace and mercy.

-Hebrews 4:16

_____
_____
_____
_____
_____
_____
_____
_____
_____
_____
_____
_____
_____

I put my trust in God when my heart is troubled.

-John 14:1

_____
_____
_____
_____
_____
_____
_____
_____
_____
_____
_____
_____

I believe you God and His words and promises..

-Matthew 19:26

_____
_____
_____
_____
_____
_____
_____
_____
_____
_____
_____
_____

I am grateful for God's son freeing me of my sins.

-John 8:36

_____
_____
_____
_____
_____
_____
_____
_____
_____
_____
_____
_____
_____
_____

I am never alone and know God is with me
and hearing my prayers.

-Philippians 1:30

I thank God for showing me the way and guiding my steps.

-Job 22:28

I thank God for loving me so much.

-Psalm 119:58

I encourage others because God inspires me to do so.

-Proverbs 11:25

_____

_____

_____

_____

_____

_____

_____

_____

_____

_____

_____

_____

_____

I know I can be brave because God is with me.

-Joshua 1:9

_____
_____
_____
_____
_____
_____
_____
_____
_____
_____
_____
_____
_____

I do not worry because I believe with all heart in God's promises.

-Isaiah 40:31

_____

_____

_____

_____

_____

_____

_____

_____

_____

_____

_____

_____

I know God's love is true, pure, and perfect.

-2 Samuel 22:31

I believe am a child of God and believe in our Lord, Jesus Christ.

-1 John 5:1

I know God will bring hope and joy to my heart when I am restless.

-Romans 15:13

_____
_____
_____
_____
_____
_____
_____
_____
_____
_____
_____
_____
_____
_____

I believe in you God and put all my hope
an trust in you.

-Isaiah 43:10

_____
_____
_____
_____
_____
_____
_____
_____
_____
_____
_____
_____

I have known God's love in good times as well as bad times – it never wavers.

-Romans 8:38

I know God is always with me and will be at my side.

-Psalm 62:5

I will make peace with my past as the Lord has instructed.

-Isaiah 43:18-19

_____

_____

_____

_____

_____

_____

_____

_____

_____

_____

_____

I know I am precious to God and for that I am not afraid.

-Daniel 10:19

I will follow the Lord's path and be a cheerful giver.

-2 Corinthians 9:7

_____
_____
_____
_____
_____
_____
_____
_____
_____
_____
_____
_____
_____

I find strength and courage' through God
and his mercy.

-Psalm 31:24

_____
_____
_____
_____
_____
_____
_____
_____
_____
_____
_____
_____
_____
_____

I turn to God when darkness descends on my heart.

-Isaiah 50:10

I place my troubles into God's hands and
know it will bring me peace.

-Romans 12:12

I am certain God's way is always the best way.

-Job 22:21

I am grateful for the amazing love and forgiveness God has given on me.

-Jude 1:2

I believe God is always with me.

-Psalm 121:1-2

I follow the path that God has made for
me with trust.

-Psalm 143:10

_____
_____
_____
_____
_____
_____
_____
_____
_____
_____
_____
_____
_____

I keep my eyes on God and know all will be well with my soul.

-1 Peter 5:10

_____
_____
_____
_____
_____
_____
_____
_____
_____
_____
_____
_____
_____
_____

I am grateful when God helps me through challenging times.

-Psalm 115:9

_____

_____

_____

_____

_____

_____

_____

_____

_____

_____

_____

_____

I will be kind and compassionate to others,
as God is to me.

-Ephesians 4:32

_____
_____
_____
_____
_____
_____
_____
_____
_____
_____
_____
_____

I am loved and blessed to be a child of God.

-1 John 4:16

I do what is right because God teaches me
through his love and wisdom.

-James 1:5

_____
_____
_____
_____
_____
_____
_____
_____
_____
_____
_____

I find peace within myself through God's teachings

-2 Thessalonians 3:16

I am grateful to God for all he has given me.

-Ephesians 1:16

I know God listens to me even before I have said a prayer.

-Isaiah 65:24

I am not afraid because I know God is protecting me from danger.

-Psalm 27:1

I see more clearly as God's light brighten my path.

-Habakkuk 3:19

I follow the Lord's teaching and trust in God's love.

-John 14:23

_____
_____
_____
_____
_____
_____
_____
_____
_____
_____
_____
_____

I am happy because I believe in God with all my heart.

-Luke 6:23

_____

_____

_____

_____

_____

_____

_____

_____

_____

_____

_____

_____

I believe in the Lord, Jesus Christ

-Isaiah 9:6

_____
_____
_____
_____
_____
_____
_____
_____
_____
_____
_____
_____
_____

I am humbled that God gave his son to take away my sins.

-1 John 4:10

_____
_____
_____
_____
_____
_____
_____
_____
_____
_____
_____

I pray because it's powerful.

-James 5:16

The Lord is my helper and I have no fear.

-Psalm 28:7

I read the scripture and God's Word
because I need them.

-2 Timothy 3:16

_____

_____

_____

_____

_____

_____

_____

_____

_____

_____

_____

I know God watches over me.

-Proverbs 15:3

I let my heart overflow with hope in the power of the Holy Spirit.

-Romans 5:5

I am confident in God's presence in my life.

-Ephesians 3:12

I feel God's compassion and love every morning when awake.

-Lamentations3:22-23

I am always comforted by God's love.

-Psalm 119:76

I know I am saved through the grace of the Lord Jesus.

-Acts 15:11

_____
_____
_____
_____
_____
_____
_____
_____
_____
_____
_____
_____
_____
_____

I know God helps me up when I fall.

-Psalm 145:14

I follow the course that God has laid out for me.

-Proverbs 16:9

_____
_____
_____
_____
_____
_____
_____
_____
_____
_____
_____
_____

I gain wisdom by following God's Word.

-Proverbs 9:9

I am not afraid because I put my faith in God.

-2 Timothy 1:7

_____
_____
_____
_____
_____
_____
_____
_____
_____
_____
_____
_____
_____

I can be bold in my faith through my trust in the Lord.

-1 John 5:14

_____

_____

_____

_____

_____

_____

_____

_____

_____

_____

_____

_____

_____

I know God watches over me and his vision
for me is perfect.

-Psalm 23:1-3

I know God will help me pick the best chooses when I ask for his help.

-Psalm 16:11

I accept God created me for a purpose that I'm still discovering.

-2 Corinthians 13:11

_____
_____
_____
_____
_____
_____
_____
_____
_____
_____
_____
_____

I believe God is always ready to help me and that I must let him.

-1 Peter 5:6-7

_____
_____
_____
_____
_____
_____
_____
_____
_____
_____
_____

I will follow God's Words today and be a friend.

-Galatians 6:2

I know nothing is impossible for me if I trust God.

-Genesis 18:14

_____

_____

_____

_____

_____

_____

_____

_____

_____

_____

_____

_____

_____

_____

I believe in God's love not only for me but for my family and friends, as well.

-Psalm 100:5

_____

_____

_____

_____

_____

_____

_____

_____

_____

_____

_____

_____

I will seek God's wisdom today.

-Proverbs 16:16

I will take care of me today and let God
carry my burden.

-Matthew 11:28

_____

_____

_____

_____

_____

_____

_____

_____

_____

_____

_____

_____

_____

I will never stop praying.

-1 Thessalonians 5:16-18

_____
_____
_____
_____
_____
_____
_____
_____
_____
_____
_____
_____
_____

I will ask God for joy and happiness today
– not just for me but for everyone.

-John 16:24

_____
_____
_____
_____
_____
_____
_____
_____
_____
_____
_____
_____
_____

I will overcome any challenges I face today,
because He will be by my side.

-1 John 5:4

_____
_____
_____
_____
_____
_____
_____
_____
_____
_____
_____

I will be guided by God today and do the work necessary to succeed.

-1 Chronicles 28:20

_____
_____
_____
_____
_____
_____
_____
_____
_____
_____
_____
_____
_____
_____

I will love others as God has taught me.

-1 John 4:11

I believe everything God has said or done is
filled with truth.

-Psalm 86:11

I will be strong today because God is always with me.

-Exodus 15:2

_____

_____

_____

_____

_____

_____

_____

_____

_____

_____

I accept my dreams are safe with God and
will move forward with confidence.

-Psalm 94:19

I will pray today and know that God is listening.

-Matthew 7:7-8

_____
_____
_____
_____
_____
_____
_____
_____
_____
_____
_____
_____
_____

I will honor God in everything I do.

-Romans 12:10

I will pray with my family today.

-Joshua 24:15

I will stay positive today and reject any negativity that comes my way.

-Hebrews 6:19

I will not let old bitter memories disturb my today.

-Colossian 3:13

_____

_____

_____

_____

_____

_____

_____

_____

_____

_____

_____

I will rejoice today for God has given me
an amazing gift.

-Psalm 97:1

_____
_____
_____
_____
_____
_____
_____
_____
_____
_____
_____
_____

I will stand strong today no matter what life throws at me.

-2 Chronicles 20:20

_____
_____
_____
_____
_____
_____
_____
_____
_____
_____
_____
_____

I will be patient today with my hopes and dreams, and even for myself.

-Romans 8:25

_____
_____
_____
_____
_____
_____
_____
_____
_____
_____
_____
_____

I know God's love for me is infinite and eternal.

-John 14:3

_____
_____
_____
_____
_____
_____
_____
_____
_____
_____
_____
_____
_____
_____

I will fill my mind with good thoughts and know my prayers will be answered..

-Philippians 4:8

_____

_____

_____

_____

_____

_____

_____

_____

_____

_____

_____

I will celebrate this day God has given me.

-John 14:27

I will help my friends be their finest selves in His name.

-1 John 4:7

_____
_____
_____
_____
_____
_____
_____
_____
_____
_____
_____
_____
_____

I will trust myself today because God already does.

-Numbers 6:24-25

I will work with passion today as if I were serving the Lord

-Ephesians 6:7

I believe in God because.. well, just because I do.

-1 John 4:12

_____
_____
_____
_____
_____
_____
_____
_____
_____
_____
_____
_____
_____

More From

GOD, Coffee & Me
Build a stronger relationship with God every morning with this prayer journal with scripture.
Type the ISBN#
1718057954
Into search
(Amazon or Google)

Take the Scripture Writing Challenge
Dig deeper into the topic of Joy and get creative with your bible study.
Type the ISBN#
1731009887
Into search
(Amazon or Google)

Made in the USA
Monee, IL
15 April 2022